I AM MR. SHORE
NOT SHORT FOR SURE

A Diversity Equity and Inclusion Statement & Bonus Annual Planner

Charlotte Elizabeth Courtenay

Copyright © 2024 by – Charlotte Elizabeth Courtenay – All Rights Reserved.

It is not legal to reproduce, duplicate, or transmit any part of this document in either electronic means or printed format. Recording of this publication is strictly prohibited.

Table of Contents

Dedication	i
Acknowledgement	ii
About the Author	iii
Forward	1
Diversity Statement	2
Annual Calendar/Weekly Planner	13

Dedication

The Sisters of St. Joseph De Cluny Nuns:

Headquarters Paris, France

Acknowledgement

My sincerest appreciation and gratitude to my dearest beloved father-in-law, Professor of Medicine Dr. G.A. Howard,

Many thanks to Project Manager Mr. James D., Account Manager Mr. Ryan H., Mr. Steve P., and the Editorial Team, the Book Cover Design Team, and the entire Team at Amazon Book Publications.

About the Author

The University of Oxford-Educated Social Scientist, Charlotte Courtenay, a New Times Best Seller, the most influential Political Strategist of our 21st Century, achieving political victories in elections for new and incumbent candidates for US Presidents and Vice Presidents, including the appointments of Cabinet Members and Supreme Court Justice Nominees, both Chambers of Congress, State Governors, UK Prime Ministers and Members of Parliament, G20 and OECD Heads of State, Heads of Multi-National Organizations, such as the Head of the UN and EU, leaders in countries and organizations such as the World Bank and IMF, University Chancellors & Presidents at institutions in our UK & USA and other leaders in countries and organizations around our world.

Forward

The title of this short book, I Am Mr. Shore: Not Short for Sure, came about as a Diversity Statement as part of an employment application to an Elite Independent Boarding School in a Mid Atlantic State. This Diversity Statement authored by Charlotte Courtenay is instrumental in reframing 'Affirmative Action,' and its ultimate reauthorization on June 29th, 2023.

Diversity Statement

The reauthorization of the miscegenation statute Plessey 1896, to the renormalization precedent statute of Brown 1954, and all subsequent like discourse redress by our Courts – Civil Rights Non-Discrimination Act of 1964, Right to Interracial Marriage Loving 1967, Free and Appropriate Public Education Act of 1975, Americans with Disabilities Act 1990, Inclusion Act 1997, Defense of Marriage Act of 1996 reauthorized with Same Sex Marriage Act of 2015 which is reauthorized with Respect for Marriage Act of 2022, is the advent of Diversity Equity and Inclusion conversation of equal rights and opportunity and education for all in our United States of America, on toward the ideals espoused in our Declaration of Independence.

Let us recognize and hold this truth in the foregoing to be self-evident. All human beings are Africans. The only thing that account for the differences in our physical appearance such as skin color has to do with the location of our recent ancestral home countries in relation to the intersecting lines of latitude and longitude with regards to distance from the Equator. Demography is simply a matter of Geography. In terms of persons who can trace their lineage back to antebellum colonial timeline, DNA may not align with physical traits, the latter which are required in the subcategories of check lists on admission applications for schools and colleges and for employment.

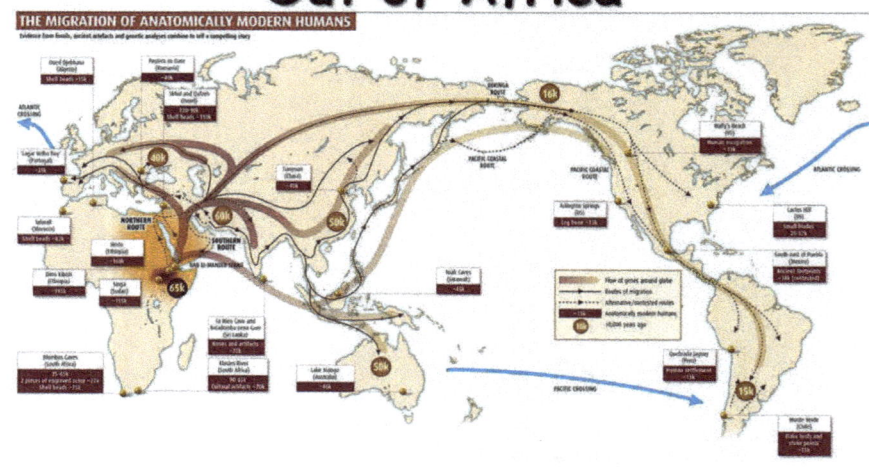
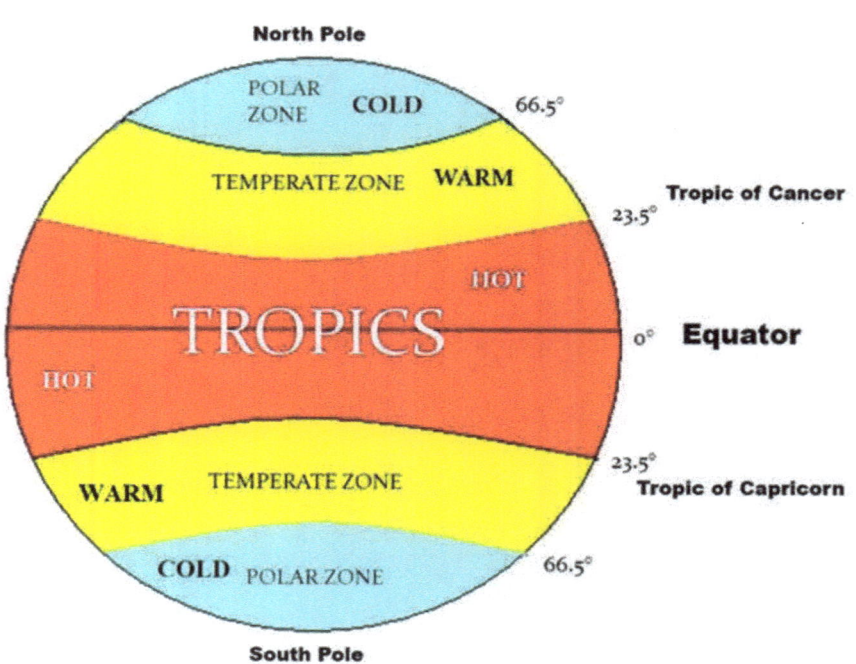

The centuries of 'passing' have created unconsciously an entire sub-category of a significant segment of our population optical illusions masquerading as persons of groups based solely on visual features rather than the substance of chromosomes. What is a man with tan skin referred to regardless unknowingly he has European Y chromosome. What is a woman with lily complexion referred to regardless unknowingly she has African Mitochondrial X chromosome. Given that we are all the sum-total of our social organization and culture – our ways of knowing and being and doing - cultural identity. We need to stand as elegant vertebrates and embrace our brethren without attaching labels intended to subaltern minority images. Let us look beyond one drop legacies, to the content of our character.

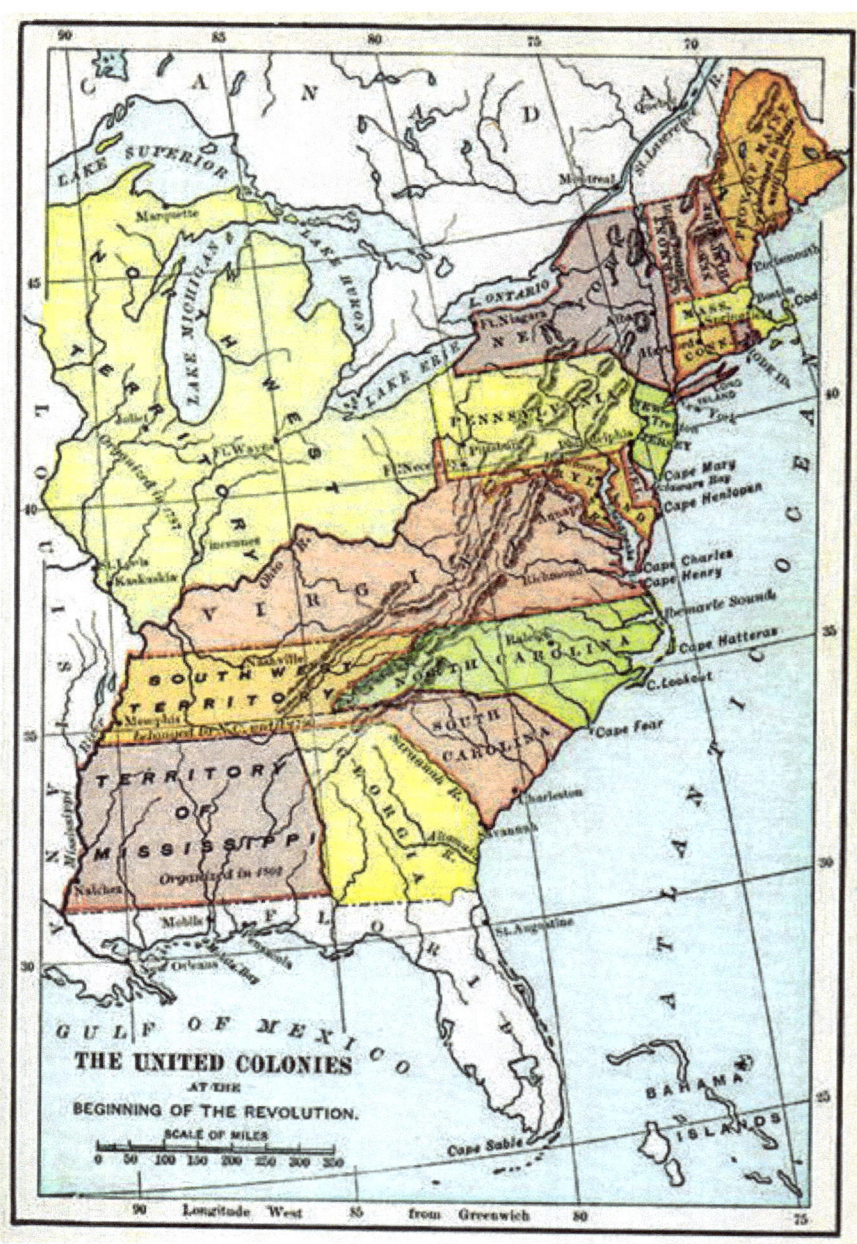

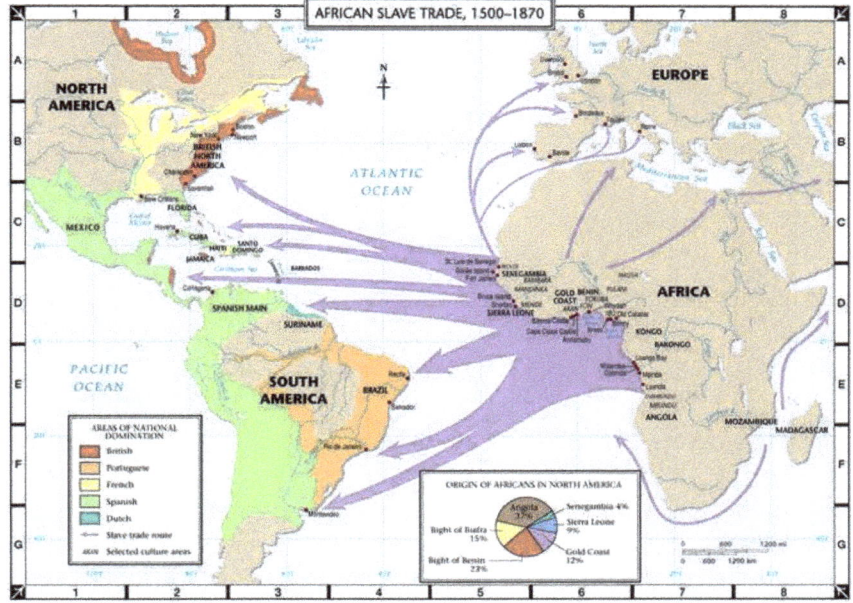

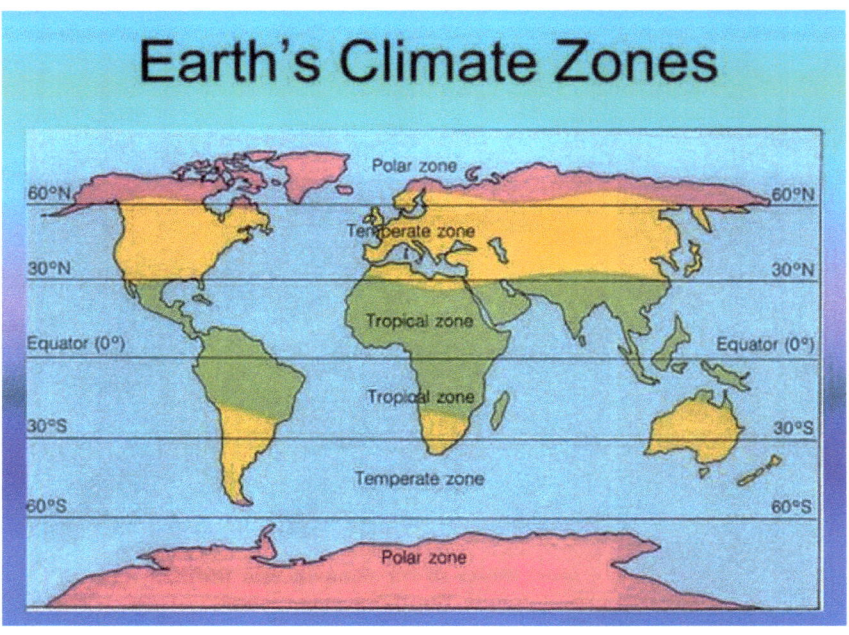

At present, the consensus discourse on Diversity Equity and Inclusion seems to advocate for a positive reverse discrimination referred to with a familiar term 'Affirmative Action.' This is not good practice for historically disadvantaged minority groups, receiving favorable treatment or the majority group denied the favorable treatment. This practice indirectly ascribes control that adversely affects the natural process of acculturation which is manufactured via these prescriptive processes of affirming some and denying others based on a set of visible physical characteristics that may not match or reflect the genetic makeup of the intended purpose of those groups whom the prescriptive programs are meant to advance. These programs also inadvertently make all those in minority groups who earned their place by their exemplary achievements into a sub-class of given a right of privilege to meet quotas, branded tokens. These policies also subjugate minority groups to become more beholden to majority groups elevated to positions of privilege and supremacy.

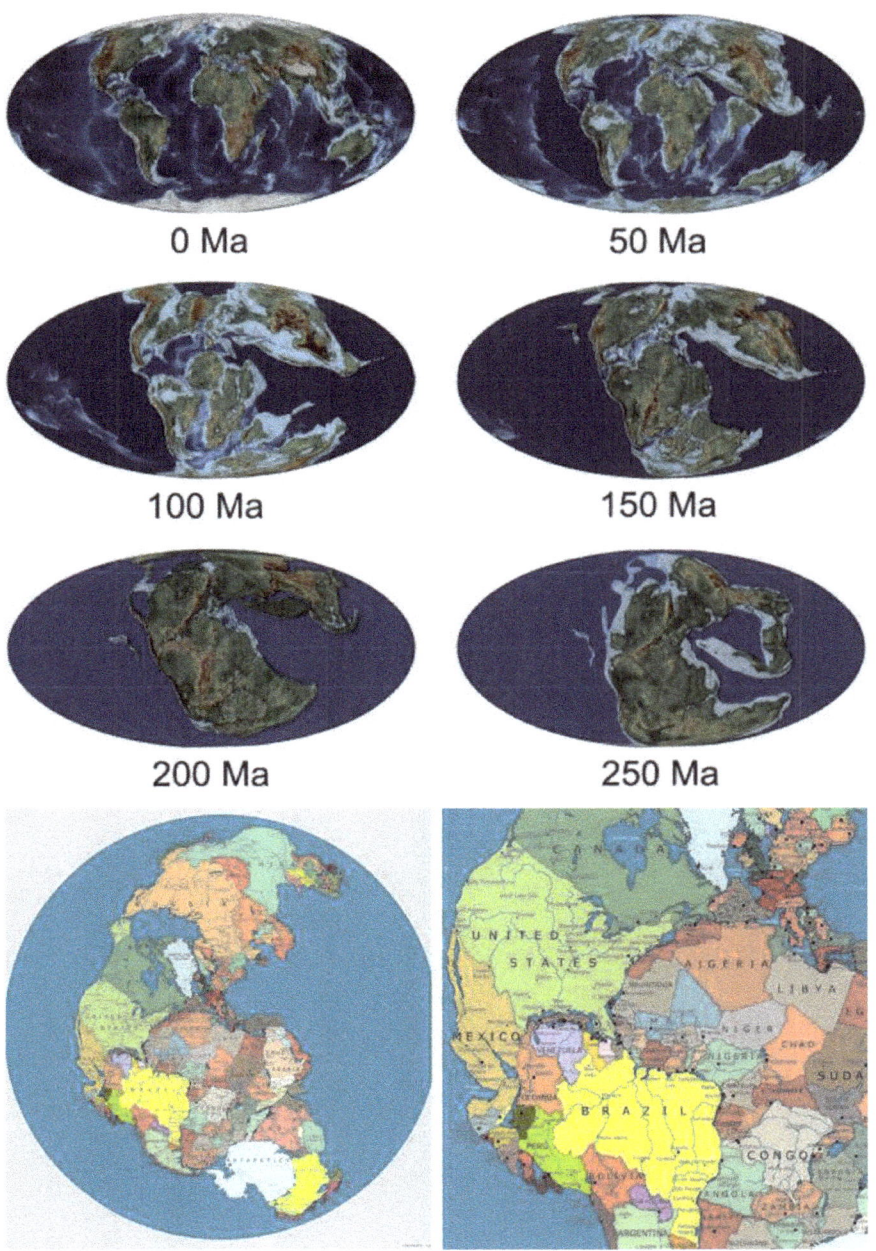

Rather than this narrow notion to remedy the realism of lasting colonial legacies, let us move ahead with the idealism that each of us are descended branches of the eternal tree created in the image and likeness of our eternal father and mother. Since our eternal father and mother reside in every sphere on our Planet Earth and in our Universe; they are a mirror reflection of all those residing within. Hence, whenever we look upon the countenance of each of our brethren, we greet and hold firming the hand and hearing the music in whatever language, taking in the scent armor of the ethnic meal we're given to sample, we recognize the face of our creator looking at us in the image and likeness of the lines of latitude and longitude in relation to the distance from the Equator wherein the topography of that geographical location, we say to thee, alas we are together again brother of mine and sister of mine created in the image of our same eternal father and mother from whence we were created then set out together some time ago, we traveled various paths to points north and south and east and west, across the surface environments of the zones of Pangea. Let us adapt to a normalization of the language and power of compassion that places the same high value and dignity on all human beings, empathy for each other, forgiveness of the past and a commitment to live in the present time, sustaining peace, building the foundation for a brighter future, with unconditional love everlasting, of and for all our Fellow Americans and Britons and Peoples around our World.

Heat Zones of the Earth

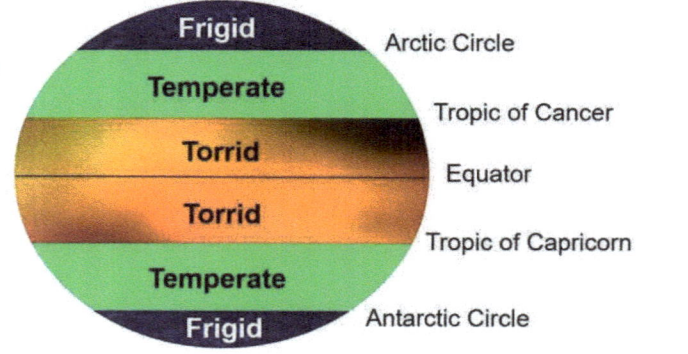

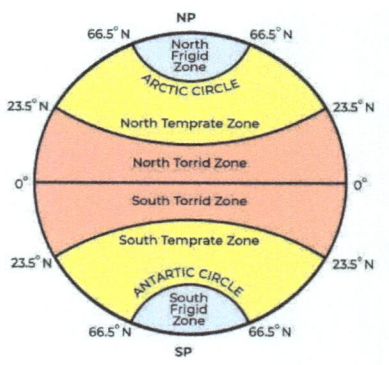

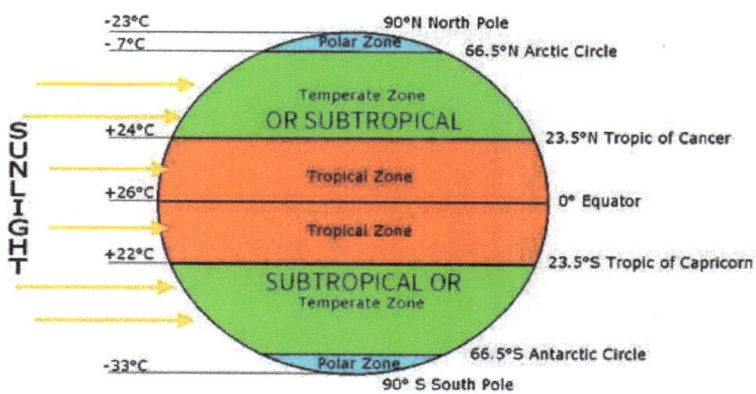

Annual Calendar/Weekly Planner

August

1	2	3	4	5	6	7
8	9	10	11	12	13	14
15	16	17	18	19	20	21
22	23	24	25	26	27	28
29	30	31				

August
First Week

Second Week

August
Third Week

Fourth Week

September

1	2	3	4	5	6	7
8	9	10	11	12	13	14
15	16	17	18	19	20	21
22	23	24	25	26	27	28
29	30					

September

First Week

Second Week

September

Third Week

Fourth Week

October

1	2	3	4	5	6	7
8	9	10	11	12	13	14
15	16	17	18	19	20	21
22	23	24	25	26	27	28
29	30	31				

October
First Week

Second Week

October
Third Week

Fourth Week

November

1	2	3	4	5	6	7
8	9	10	11	12	13	14
15	16	17	18	19	20	21
22	23	24	25	26	27	28
29	30					

November
First Week

Second Week

November
Third Week

Fourth Week

December

1	2	3	4	5	6	7
8	9	10	11	12	13	14
15	16	17	18	19	20	21
22	23	24	25	26	27	28
29	30	31				

December

First Week

Second Week

December

Third Week

Fourth Week

January

1	2	3	4	5	6	7
8	9	10	11	12	13	14
15	16	17	18	19	20	21
22	23	24	25	26	27	28
29	30	31				

January
First Week

Second Week

January
Third Week

Fourth Week

February

1	2	3	4	5	6	7
8	9	10	11	12	13	14
15	16	17	18	19	20	21
22	23	24	25	26	27	28
29						

February
First Week

Second Week

February
Third Week

Fourth Week

March

1	2	3	4	5	6	7
8	9	10	11	12	13	14
15	16	17	18	19	20	21
22	23	24	25	26	27	28
29	30	31				

March

First Week

Second Week

March
Third Week

Fourth Week

April

1	2	3	4	5	6	7
8	9	10	11	12	13	14
15	16	17	18	19	20	21
22	23	24	25	26	27	28
29	30					

April

First Week

Second Week

April
Third Week

Fourth Week

May

1	2	3	4	5	6	7
8	9	10	11	12	13	14
15	16	17	18	19	20	21
22	23	24	25	26	27	28
29	30	31				

May

First Week

Second Week

May

Third Week

Fourth Week

June

1	2	3	4	5	6	7
8	9	10	11	12	13	14
15	16	17	18	19	20	21
22	23	24	25	26	27	28
29	30					

June
First Week

Second Week

June
Third Week

Fourth Week

July

1	2	3	4	5	6	7	
8	9	10	11	12	13	14	
15	16	17	18	19	20	21	
22	23	24	25	26	27	28	
29	30	31					

July
First Week

Second Week

July

Third Week

Fourth Week

www.ingramcontent.com/pod-product-compliance
Lightning Source LLC
Chambersburg PA
CBHW040242130526
44590CB00049B/4208